Glorifying God,
Centered in Christ,
Stepping with the Spirit

Glorifying God,
Centered in Christ,
Stepping with the Spirit

A Spiritual Feast

Edwin Yip

RESOURCE *Publications* • Eugene, Oregon

GLORIFYING GOD, CENTERED IN CHRIST, STEPPING WITH THE SPIRIT
A Spiritual Feast

Copyright © 2020 Edwin Yip. All rights reserved. Except for brief quotations in critical publications or reviews, no part of this book may be reproduced in any manner without prior written permission from the publisher. Write: Permissions, Wipf and Stock Publishers, 199 W. 8th Ave., Suite 3, Eugene, OR 97401.

Resource Publications
An Imprint of Wipf and Stock Publishers
199 W. 8th Ave., Suite 3
Eugene, OR 97401

www.wipfandstock.com

PAPERBACK ISBN: 978-1-7252-7728-1
HARDCOVER ISBN: 978-1-7252-7727-4
EBOOK ISBN: 978-1-7252-7729-8

Manufactured in the U.S.A.   09/11/20

Contents

Preface | vii
Acknowledgement | ix

CHRISTMAS Is Here | 1
God Loves Us | 2
Worshipping the Lord | 3
Good Enough | 5
Navigator | 7
The View from Above | 9
O Faithful One | 11
The Lord's Helping Hand | 13
Low Moments | 15
Draw Me Near | 17
In You | 18
A Song Poem | 20
Connected | 21
Sometimes | 23
I Remember | 24
Don't Ever Forget God | 26
I Have Been Called | 27

Voice of God | 29
Learning Curve | 30
Truth and Lies | 32
In My Midst | 34
Time Worth Spending | 36
Heart to Heart | 38
Heartache | 41
The God Who Acts | 43
Mighty | 45
Undying Fire | 47
Faith beyond Belief | 49
The Lord Is | 51
Soak in His Presence | 52
Life a See-Saw | 54
I Can Trust God | 56

Extra Poems | 59
 Homebound | 62
 COVID-19 | 63

Songs List | 65

Preface

I CANNOT BEGIN TO describe my excitement and amazement when this project entered its final stages. From a young age, I dreamt of becoming an author, but it was epic fantasy that I enjoyed reading. Therefore, I had always wanted to write books in this specific genre. But God turned my attention away, and in January 2016 during a short-term mission trip, he ignited my desire to glorify him through my poetry.

I went through several years of doubt and wrestled with the idea of wanting to become a published poet. I asked myself, "Is it my own ambition, or is it a calling that God places in my heart, in order to glorify him?"

When the Lord said this to me, can I be any more emboldened?

> *The poetry will be of good news. Keep writing. I am with you as you write them so don't worry . . . You do your part and I will do my part. Just stick to the truth, which is my voice, and you will be fine.*

In the process to reach publication, God encouraged me further with the following words.

> *Listen, child*
> *I am not done with you yet*
> *I have not finished what I started*
> *You are my beloved son*
>
> *Peace I leave with you*
> *Listen to my voice*
> *Even in the storm*
> *And all will be well*
>
> *Never give up*
> *For I am with you*
> *Beside you daily*
> *And you know me*

May you find encouragement, peace, and joy also, as you choose to dwell in the shelter of our Lord Most High.

Acknowledgement

I WOULD LIKE TO thank my family, friends, and brothers and sisters in Christ who have supported and encouraged me in this journey. I would especially like to mention Charmaine, Deborah, Derek, Jonathan, and Shirley. Thank you for all your hours spent listening to and reading over my poems. Finally yet importantly, I want to dedicate this work to my Lord Jesus Christ, whom through his grace and mercy answered my prayers.

CHRISTMAS Is Here

Dear Congregation
Christmas is here, Christ has Come
Let us Celebrate Christ
The Cornerstone of all Churches

Holy is He in the Highest
Let us lift up our Hands
Let us sing Hallelujah
Like the Heavenly Hosts

Rejoice! You who have been Redeemed
And Reconciled through Christ
In Reverent fear we praise
Let us Reflect God's glory

I adore you, Jesus
I love you, Jesus
I give you my life, Jesus
I submit to you, Jesus

In Spirit
  and Truth
    we worship you, the Messiah

Alle-lu-ia, Alle-lu-ia, Alle-lu-ia
Alle-lu-ia, Alle-lu-ia, Alle-lu-ia

Let us Sing together!

Alle-lu-ia, Alle-lu-ia, Alle-lu-ia
Alle-lu-ia, Alle-lu-ia, Alle-lu-ia

Merry C-H-R-I-S-T-M-A-S

God Loves Us

I am filling myself with the love of God's grace
A reminder that draws on God's character
If you think about how amazing our God is
We should be utterly speechless

We are so easily tainted by the world around us
So easily forgetful of the good done by an invisible God
So easily focused on the might of man, a hollow boast

We worship not because God is vain or that he needs it
But it reminds us not to forget who he is
In the same way, we pray not because God doesn't know our situations
Or that he needs us to pray to him
But it helps us to focus on the truth
Who he is and why he cares

And if you ask why he cares
That's because he loves us
And that is the reason we are here today
To get to know God better
Through each other's support

Remember, nothing can separate us from him
God *loves* us. Do you believe that as the truth?

Worshipping the Lord

I step up to the altar
My palms clasped in prayer
My eyes fixed on the cross
I worship you, my Lord

This is my posture
  with head bowed
    knees bent
    arms high
    heart wide
  and my soul cries

You are the Lord Al-mighty
You are the Lord All-worthy
You are the Lord All-eternity
You are my Lord Al-ways
And I worship you

We come together united
Your presence hovers over us
Your Spirit is palpable in the air
We shout praises to your name

This is our posture
  with heads bowed
    knees bent
    arms high
    hearts wide
  and our souls cry

You are the Lord Al-mighty
You are the Lord All-worthy
You are the Lord All-eternity
You are our Lord Al-ways
And we worship you

Father, you adopted us
As yours
Jesus, you died on the cross
For us
Spirit, you came to lead us
To you
And we worship you

The Lord Al-mighty is All-worthy for All-eternity
And we worship him Al-ways

Good Enough

Sometimes I wonder if I am worthy
To be a child of God
To come into your presence
To be among the saints

The voices that lie
Tell me I am not good enough
The values set by the world
That's not who I am

My value never changes
Redeemed by the cross
Your voice never lies
Tell me I am good enough

I am GOOD enough
I am GOOD enough

Let your mercy burn into my soul
No second thoughts
No second thoughts

I am GOOD enough
I am GOOD enough

Freed from the bondage of slavery
The voices that tell me lies
The values set by the world
That's not who I am

I am *now* a child of God
Redeemed by the cross
Adopted as one in Christ
That's who I am

I am GOOD enough
I am GOOD enough

Let your mercy burn into my soul
No second thoughts
No second thoughts

A privilege to be yours
Let me serve you wholeheartedly
No second thoughts
No second thoughts

I am always GOOD enough
I will always be GOOD enough

I am a child of God
Redeemed by the cross
Adopted as one in Christ
That's who I am

Navigator

Lord, I am lost
I am not sure which road to pick
There are so many paths ahead
So many strings pulling me
So many things capture my heart
Taking my attention away from you

Who is my Navigator?
It's not me
It's not the world
It's you, God, my Personal Savior

The GPS I rely on is true
Never changing from the beginning
To the very end, it stays the same

The GPS I rely on is personal
It knows me by my name
It calls out to me and lifts me by my arms

The GPS I rely on is mighty
Nothing can compare to him
It delivers me through a time, time and again

God, my Personal Savior
It blows my mind even to think about it
You are the Creator of the universe
Yet you want a relationship with me
Yet you sacrificed yourself to be my Savior

Lord, how can I possibly respond
To this good news
Except to make you my Navigator
From now on till my death
Which is not the end

I am no longer lost
I may not know the exact path
But I trust in my GPS
God, my Personal Savior

The View from Above

I look up at the silhouette of the mountain
At the shadow of the passing eagle
Oh, how I wish to be up there
To see the view from above

Step by step I climb
Struggling up the slope
Battered by the tempest
I fall . . . only to stand again

I am drawn to the light on the mountain
I am sheltered by the shadow under his wings
I carry on

Step by step I climb
Struggling up the slope
Battered by the tempest
I fall . . . only to stand again

It's all worth it in the end
The view from above, oh, how I long for it
To see with clarity, God's
Orchestration

Do you see it?
Do you yearn for it?
It's all around you
The blessings from above

O Heaven's Grace, Merciful Love
It's lavished freely upon the world
Christ's blood, the sacrificial lamb

Do you see it?
Do you yearn for it?
It's all around you
The blessings from above

I am here, I am standing strong
On the peak of a mountain
On the back of an eagle
My God, my God, I praise you!

How I long to stay here
So I can see with clarity
The view from a mountain's peak
The view from an eagle's back
The view from above

Yes, Lord, I have tasted and seen you are good
My heart craves for more spiritual food
For I know there is an even higher mountain peak
And the eagle can fly straight to heaven still
Oh, how I wish to hear you speak
So I may discern your good, pleasing, and perfect will
Let me dwell in the house of the Lord forever

O Faithful One

Into the darkness of despair, I cry my soul
From the shadow of my sins, you pull me out

You are my light
You are my hope
You are my faithful one, Lord

You are my light
You are my hope
You are my faithful one, Lord

Wherever I go, you are with me
Whatever I do, you are forever here
That's right, O Lord

You are my light
You are my hope
You are my faithful one, Lord

You are my light
You are my hope
You are my faithful one, Lord

Let the world rejoice at your presence
Let the world shout your magnificence
Let the world worship you
O faithful one, O faithful one

From grace I have fallen, yet I need not be afraid
You are forever with me, Lord of the heavens

You are my light
You are my hope
You are my faithful one, Lord

You are my light
You are my hope
You are my faithful one, Lord

Wherever I go, you are with me
Whatever I do, you are forever here
That's right, O Lord

You are my light
You are my hope
You are my faithful one, Lord

You are my light
You are my hope
You are my faithful one, Lord

Let the world rejoice at your presence
Let the world shout your magnificence
Let the world worship you
O faithful one, O faithful one

O faithful one, O faithful one

The Lord's Helping Hand

We see the world through your eyes
The poor and needy cry for help
The need is great but you are greater
Your love has no boundary

Help us see and open our ears
Help us feel and move our hearts
Help us go and be your hands
Lord, help us Lord, help us be your hands!

We are the Lord's servants
By your mighty hand we were saved
Strengthen us now so we may go
And be your hands and feet

Strengthen us now so we may go
And be your hands and feet

The widow and the fatherless
The poor and the foreigner
They cry out in their distress
Under oppression they seek justice

Help us see and open our ears
Help us feel and move our hearts
Help us go and be your hands
Lord, help us Lord, help us be your hands!

We are the Lord's servants
By your mighty hand we were saved
Strengthen us now so we may go
And be your hands and feet

Strengthen us now so we may go
And be your hands and feet

Your hand is power and might
It is from on high
All of us are the works of your hand
Uphold us with your righteous right hand

Low Moments

Sometimes I want to give up
Yeah, you know what I mean

When my body is full of burdens
When my mind is muddled with doubts
When my soul is weary with sorrows
How I wish to just give up

Forget about God. Forget about Jesus.
Just live out my own freedom

They say, you say, I say, this
Who should I listen to?

I want to turn away from you, Lord
That's what I see people doing
That's what the world is doing
But deep down a part of me refuses

Even though my body is burdened
Even though my mind is muddled
Even though my soul is sorrowful
A part of me refuses

I want to give up
You know what I mean
A part of me refuses
Why do I still care about God?

It's because of this
Jesus Christ died on the cross (for me)
And resurrected
He will return to be crowned King

Is this an everyday matter?
Dying on the cross for the sake of others?
He set the precedence
Yet our hearts remain stubborn

I cannot forget history
I cannot pretend it never happened
I cannot remain stoic
Maybe it's the Holy Spirit inside me
Stirring my heart

Yeah, you know what I mean

From morning till evening
My eyes are fixed on you
Jesus Christ, my Lord
He is my everything
I surrender my all

Jesus Christ, my Lord
He is my everything
I surrender my all

Jesus Christ, my Lord
He is my everything
I surrender my all

Draw Me Near

I wash my hands and purify my heart
For I am a sinner and double minded
Forgive me, Lord, when I run from your embrace
When I flee towards temptation

Help me submit to you
Help me resist evil

For I wish nothing more than to draw near
To draw near to you, Lord

Draw me near through your grace
Draw me near into your embrace
Draw me near so I may face
Everything through your loving grace

In your presence I submit
To the devil I refuse

For I wish nothing more than to draw near
Than to draw near to you, Lord

Draw me near through your grace
Draw me near into your embrace
Draw me near that I may face
Everything through your love and grace

In You

Oh Lord, search me and know my heart
For I am eager to abide

In You I find love
In You I find joy
In You I find peace
In You I find patience
In You I find kindness
In You I find goodness
In You I find faithfulness
In You I find gentleness
In You I find self-control

In You I find an abundant life
Everlasting
Even when evil is rife
In a world that is falling apart
And full of strife

My faith remains in you
Jesus Christ, my Lord

My hope remains in you
Holy Spirit, my Lord

My love remains in you
Sovereign God, my Lord

In You I find an abundant life
Everlasting
Even when evil is rife
In a world that is falling apart
And full of strife

I will come to you and find rest
For I thirst for water that quenches
And food that satisfies my hunger
Best

No one can compare to you
Who is greater than you?
In You I trust
For you have never forsaken us

Thank you, Lord Almighty
You are worthy of all praises
May your name be glorified
Now and forevermore

A Song Poem

(*See Songs List, 65*)

Grace, because of who you are
I give you my heart
I am not ashamed
To be like Jesus

Yes, Lord, yes
This I believe
You are, more, greater still
Worthy of worship

Praise the King
Forever reign, above all
Blessed be your name
Jesus Messiah

You are my all in all
Wonderful, merciful Savior
No longer slaves, I will rise
Like eagles, trust in you

I want to be just like you
Carry the light, build a bridge of love
Freely, freely, by faith
For the glory of the Lord

You are holy, awesome God
Draw me close to you
Lead me to the cross
In Christ alone, I will stand

Solid rock, unshakeable
Your love never fails
I can only imagine, what faith can do
In the name of the Lord

Connected

Am I far or am I near?
Am I moving towards or away?
Is my heart beating in sync?
Is my soul resting in peace?
Am I connected?

Is it not . . .
Through the words of God
The meditation of my heart
And my commitment to obey

Is it not . . .
Through praising God
As I lift up my hands in surrender
And dedicate my soul undivided

Is it not . . .
Through prayers to God
About anything and everything
Trusting in his goodness patiently

Only then am I connected
With the power to control and banish my evil thoughts
So I may behave in a manner pleasing to him

Connected like an umbilical cord
Between a mother and her child
Oh, let your gracious love flood towards me
Constantly renewing my strength

My sinful self fades away
Transforming into his likeness
Through the power of the cord
Constantly recycling my waste

Oh, how I wish to stay connected
Through prayers and praises
Through perusing and pondering
The words and works of God!

May the grace of the Lord Jesus Christ
The love of God
And the fellowship of the Holy Spirit
Be with all those who seek him earnestly
Forever, and ever, and evermore

Sometimes

Sometimes I wish I was more courageous
God did not give us a spirit of timidity
Do I want heaven without you?
It might be too late then

Sometimes I wish I was wiser
God promised to give us what we ask in faith
Do I want heaven without you?
It is so easy for me to remain silent

Sometimes I wish I was more eloquent
When I do not know what to say
Let your Spirit speak in my stead
Do you think God wants heaven without you?

Sometimes I wish I was less hypocritical
But I am only human, so I stumble
Yes, it is grace that is at work
The same grace that is given freely for all

Sometimes I wish I was stronger
In all that I do for Christ
Maybe then, people could see and wonder
And seek God on their own initiative

Sometimes I wish I was more compassionate
To see you as God sees you
But how often do I turn a blind eye
And let my own thoughts and emotions dictate my actions?

Sometimes I wish I was more loving
We love because he first loved us
Let's face it
Is it sometimes, nevertimes, or oftentimes?

I Remember

It was meant to be a day like any other
From the morning that should be bright
It was shrouded in mist and fire instead

When you lose something you shouldn't lose
When you break something you shouldn't break
When it's not you, but those around you
When nothing seems like it will ever work out
... That kind of day

The frustration builds
The anger simmering inside
The short fuse temper shows
There is an urge to start pointing fingers
... But then I remember

I remember how he did it
Every right not to be condemned
Every right to justify and prove us wrong
Every right not to suffer from guilt, shame, nor fear
... He humbled himself

He chose not to hide
He chose not to strike back
He chose not to use his rights

The world teaches us differently
Who is your master?
Whom do we follow?

When frustration builds
How should we respond?
In kind or with kindness

Remember what he did
He took our sins
So we may be free
Live a life born again

The wine and the bread
We remember, oh how we remember
The price he paid, for each of us
. . . It is finished

Don't Ever Forget God

Amazing grace
Broken pieces that we are
Christ sacrificed himself for us

So Don't Ever Forget God!

Almighty is our Lord
Boundless in his knowledge
Creator of this universe

So Don't Ever Forget God!

Abounding in love, slow to anger
Blessed is our Lord
Compassionate beyond doubt

So Don't Ever Forget God!

Always there, ever present
Beside his children, protecting
Closely watching, never resting

So Don't Ever Forget God!

Able to heal all brokenness
Bringing us deeper into his embrace
Calling us to draw near to him

So Don't Ever Forget God!

Adopted as sons and daughters
Bravely we call him Abba
Christ is our Lord and King

I Have Been Called

I have been called
By the Lord of lords, King of kings
The love of God
Embraces me

I have been saved
By the Lord of lords, King of kings
The grace of Jesus Christ
Washes over me

I have been marked
By the Lord of lords, King of kings
The fellowship of the Holy Spirit
Dwells in me

Lord of lords, King of kings
We praise you for what you have done
The wonders of your creation
The mysteries of your salvation
Lord of lords, King of kings
You have called me
You have saved me
You have marked me
What more can I say

Lord of lords, King of kings
We turn our hearts from you
We trust in our strength
We fall without knowing
Lord of lords, King of kings
Yet you called me
Yet you saved me
Yet you marked me
What more can I say

I have been called
I have been saved
I have been marked
By the Lord of lords, King of kings

I have been called
I have been saved
I have been marked
By the Lord of lords, King of kings
What more can I say

Voice of God

You call me by my name at this present time
A whisper in my ears, a vision in my mind
Your Spirit is the messenger of truth and love

The people around me come
A gentle word, and gesture of kindness here and there
I feel blessed, truly blessed

The words flow forth from within my heart
The Spirit groans alongside my prayers, and
The voices of those beyond my hearing

You listen from high above
Everything is within your sovereign grace
I surrender my life and my health into your hands

Heal me quick if that is thy will
Heal me slow if that achieves more for your kingdom's sake
That is my request

Learning Curve

I was once a baby
I did not walk from day one
I did not eat solids from the start
I did not rely on myself

I stumble and fall
I choke and cry
I look to my loving parents
To learn and thrive

It's a learning curve
And it's no different now that I am reborn
Thanks to the acts of my Savior

It's not natural for me to run first
Neither can I handle solids from the start
It's naturnal to rely on another

Though He is like no other
Like our loving parents
He extends the olive branch
Treated like a royal child
Wiped clean from our mistakes
Nothing held against us

We stumble and fall
We choke and cry
We look to our Heavenly Father
To learn and thrive

It's no different
I was and am once a baby
Physically and spiritually
It's a learning curve

Thanks be to our Father
For his endless grace and patience
And his everlasting love
Let's learn to take the right steps
Spiritually
And it's okay to stumble

Truth and Lies

Do not entertain evil
Do not give him even an inch
Give him a foothold and he will dig into your soul
Eagerly devouring the truth
And muttering lies non-stop

Lies so simple
Lies so subtle
Lies so bold
That we often fall for it

We can't fight this battle on our own
And thankfully we do not need to

We have a stronger partner by our side
The Holy Spirit ever present
Beside each of our souls
Uttering nothing but the truth
The voice of God

Truth so profound
Truth so real
Truth so healing
That we often cry from hearing it

Let us learn to step with the Spirit
The power given us to resist
It rejoices with the truth
And denounces all lies

There is nowhere left to hide
The darkness revealed by the light
The evil that trembles at the good
The sins washed by the blood
Of Jesus Christ
He speaks the truth, the word of God
And that, is all we need to hear

In My Midst

It's the truth
When I wake up in bed ready for the day
It's the truth
Whether I am thinking, doing, working or not
It's the truth
Whether I am playing, resting, sleeping or not
It's the truth
When I lie down in bed tired from the day
It's the truth

You are in my midst
Now and forevermore
In laughter and in sorrows
Through peace or struggles
Never a day short

It's the truth
You are in my midst

True and unforgettable
More than just a whisper in my head
More than just a fragment of my mind
It's the truth

True and overwhelming
More than I can ever imagine
More than I can ever understand
It's the truth

True and present every day
More than just a figure of history
More than just a King yet to come
It's the truth

You are in my midst
Now and forevermore
In laughter and in sorrows
Through peace or struggles
Never a day short

It's the truth
You are in my midst

You are more, you are more
The God of unforgettable grace
It's amazing, amazing grace
You are more, you are more
The God of overwhelming love
It's reckless, reckless love
You are more, you are more
Than just the God who is present every day

You died for me while I was still a sinner
You were for me when I was against you
So now, why do I worry?

It's the truth
This is who our Lord is
This is who is in our midst!

Time Worth Spending

I could have chosen otherwise
But it's time worth spending
To be with you Lord
To be in your presence
To be in your embrace

Holy One
Your comfort, your warmth, your tenderness
I desire them all
I desire to know you better
So I may reflect your mercy and love
To those around me

Life choices are many, daily
Some insignificant, some life-changing
It could be a series of decisions
Down a slippery slope
Or many seeds of righteousness
Planted
Waiting for harvest

It's a choice
And we have the freedom to choose

I could have chosen otherwise
But it's time worth spending
To be with you Lord
To be in your presence
To be in your embrace

You are my Savior
Not aloof but near
Your suffering, your sacrifice, your obedience
I desire to understand
I desire to never forget
The price you paid for us

You sent a gift after ascension
The Holy Spirit among us
Your guidance, your voice, your truth
I desire to hear you speak
I desire to obey your words
Nothing compares in value to your Book

Forgive me, Lord, when I have chosen unwisely
It's a learning curve still in progress

I could have chosen otherwise
But it's time worth spending
To be with you Lord
To be in your presence
To be in your embrace

May it be so

Heart to Heart

"ba-dum"
"ba-dum"
"ba-dum"

"ba-dum"
"ba-dum"
"ba-dum"

Can you hear the heartbeat?
The Spirit alive
God is with us

"ba-dum"
"ba-dum"
"ba-dum"

"ba-dum"
"ba-dum"
"ba-dum"

Can you hear the heartbeat?
The unity in Christ
God's people together

"ba-dum"
"ba-dum"
"ba-dum"

"ba-dum"
"ba-dum"
"ba-dum"

It's heart to heart
God loves us first
We love God in return
Love spills everywhere

"ba-dum"
"ba-dum"
"ba-dum"

It's heart to heart
God calls us here
We answer in response
His will in everything

"ba-dum"
"ba-dum"
"ba-dum"

It's heart to heart
God sends us forth
We obey his commands
Share the news to everyone

"ba-dum"
"ba-dum"
"ba-dum"

"ba-dum"
"ba-dum"
"ba-dum"

Can you hear the heartbeat?
He fashions us in our mothers' wombs
We each have a purpose
A calling to fulfill

"ba-dum"
"ba-dum"
"ba-dum"

"ba-dum"
"ba-dum"
"ba-dum"

Can you hear your heartbeat?

"ba-dum"
"ba-dum"
"ba-dum"

Who is beating alongside it?

"ba-dum"
"ba-dum"
"ba-dum"

Who is at the center of our hearts?

Heartache

This might be a typical day at the office
How my heart aches
How much more our Heavenly Father does too

I want to reach out
I want to shout across
A simple truth
Oh, how God loves you
Don't say such things
Carelessly
Life is not meaningless

The other day it was a 16-year-old boy
Today it was a 13-year-old girl
Last week it was an elderly man
And this week may be a woman in her prime
All contemplating an end
An end to life

There were also those seeking terminations
For their unborn babies
And many more that willingly
Harm their bodies

Oh, how my heart aches
How much more our Heavenly Father does too

I want to reach out
I want to shout across
A simple truth
Oh, how God loves you
Don't say such things
Carelessly
Life is not meaningless

Though the world might seem bleak
And full of hatred and sufferings
There is beauty, and love, and joy
To be sought

Jesus is the way
Revealed through the Spirit
By the grace of God

It's beyond my control
I know you care
BREAK THEIR CHAINS, O LORD

Lift them from their darkness
Show them the light
A shining anchor that guides their paths
A simple truth

The God Who Acts

You were never far but always near by my side
You were gracious enough to stay when I left your side
In my moments of weakness that you already knew
You forgave me before I even turned away

Gently but persistently, you called out
Beckoning and drawing me back to you
You held no grudge but with arms wide open
Rejoicing in the return of every sinner

Again and again, you prove to be present and alive
You are the God who acts
So we lift up our hands and sing
Glory to your name, the name
Above all names

You were never far but always near by my side
You were ready to support me when I fell to the side
In my moments of struggle that you already knew
You pulled me through so I could stand strong

In faith and hope, I put my trust in you
Remembering your promises to deliver
You held back nothing good from me
Blessing me according to your perfect will

Again and again, you prove to be present and alive
You are the God who acts
So we lift up our hands and sing
Glory to your name, the name
Above all names

Open our eyes, tune our ears
Open our eyes, tune our ears
Let us see, let us hear
Let us see, let us hear
The acts of God, the God who acts!

Mighty

Mighty is our Lord
Mighty is the one who holds it all

Everything is in his hands
In his wisdom
In his love
In his grace
He pours out his mercy

Not a single hair less
Not a single sparrow short
He knows them all
Just as he knows us all

Every soul in heaven and earth
Under his care
Dead or alive
He knows them all

Mighty is our Lord
Mighty is the one who holds it all

Everything is in his hands
The day is coming
When in his great wisdom
In his great truth
In his great holiness
He will pour out his justice

May that day come soon
But not before we are ready

Repent
   Repent
      Repent

Hold on to our faith

Share
   Share
      Share

Spread the good news!

For mighty is our Lord
Mighty is the one who holds it all

Undying Fire

There is a fire in my soul
Burning brightly as it should
No matter what comes
It will never be snuffed out

Laugh all you want
Sneer while you can
Mock if you like
It ain't affecting me

There is a fire burning in my soul
You place it there, O Lord
You are my sustainer
And it will never be snuffed out

We are the lamp
You are the source
We burn brightly as we should
You sustain us through the Spirit

There is a fire burning in my soul
Burning brightly as it should
No matter what comes
It will never be snuffed out

Lies you can whisper
Mud you can throw
Walls you can build
It ain't affecting me

Jesus
You are the God of truth
Paving a path across obstacles
Walls crumble in your name

Nothing can stand against us
For you, O Lord, is our source
There is a fire burning in our souls
Setting ablaze the world as it spreads

Faith beyond Belief

I asked the Lord the other day
What does it mean to have "a leap of faith"?
Four words he placed in my mind
Humble, surrender, willing, obedience

Are we humble, in front of our God?
Are we in control of our lives,
Or do we surrender it all to our Lord?
Are we willing to serve, to make sacrifices, to take up our cross daily,
Not for our benefits but for those around us?
Are we obedient to the word of God,
Heading in the direction he called us to?

Humble, surrender, willing, obedience

Lord, it's not easy. It's impossible without your Spirit
A leap of faith is faith beyond belief

We believe in God our Heavenly Father
We believe in the death and resurrection of the Son
He is Jesus Christ
We believe in the Holy Spirit
Our God three in one

We believe in miracles
We believe he is here
Beside us daily
We believe he has prepared a home
For us to return to

We believe all that
But it's easier to proclaim what we believe
Than it is to act in faith

Lord, let this be our prayers
To be humble
To surrender ourselves
To be willing
To be obedient
To have faith

The Lord Is

The Lord is my King
He judges me for who I am
Evil he despises, mercy for the righteous

The Lord is my Shield
He protects me from harm's way
My rock, my fortress, my savior

The Lord is my Star
He guides me through the course of life
The path to righteousness, for his name's sake

The Lord is my Cure
He heals me from the bottom up
My soul he cleanses, makes pure in his eyes

The Lord is my Builder
He provides me with all I need
To strengthen and equip, for the battle ahead

The Lord is my Father
In heaven and on earth
His will be done
I will serve him forever and ever more

Soak in His Presence

I simply come
To soak in your presence
Staying still
Embedded in worship
Let my thoughts stay behind
Amongst the chorus
Focus on you alone

I simply come
To soak in your presence
Laying still
Embedded in worship
Let my fears run away
Joining in
Focus on you alone

From being still
To making noises
I simply come
Leave my thoughts behind
Approach the throne
Raise my voice
To praise you alone

I simply come
To stand still
Soak in your presence
Worshipping
Amongst the chorus
Listening
Every tongue confess
Every knee bowing

From being still
To making noises
I simply come
Leave my thoughts behind
Approach the throne
Raise my voice
To praise you alone

I simply come
To soak in your presence
Staying still
And worshipping

I simply come
To soak in your presence
Laying still
And worshipping

I simply come
To soak in your presence
Standing still
And worshipping

Life a See-Saw

Here I am again
Hiding from your presence
Gripped with shame, guilt, and fear
I thought I was heading
In the right direction
Only to find myself
Sliding in the wrong direction

Life is a see-saw
And you know it well
I am only from dust
And to dust I will return
You have been through it all
And so you know
You understand our weaknesses

The devastating truth is this
I will always be a sinner
No matter how much I try

The wonderful truth is this
God will always be merciful
No matter how much I sin

If I call Jesus my Lord
If I believe he rose from the dead
If I do not profane the Holy Spirit
But confess my sins
In faith and in truth
He Will FORGIVE

Lord, O Lord
Forgive me and wash me anew
Your mercy each morning renew
Refresh by your heavenly dew
I will praise you, O Lord
With all my heart

For you walked the face of the earth
The only sinless man
Obedient to the cross
Jesus, my King and Savior
I will glorify your name forever
Among the people, among the nations

I will glorify your name forever
Among the people, and among the nations
I will sing praises to your name
With all my heart

I Can Trust God

My greatest fear
Is that one day I will turn away from
You Lord
I cannot swear
I cannot guarantee
That I will never renounce my faith

It's my human nature
I can't trust myself
That it will never happen
But I can trust God

He is always merciful
He is always there beside me
He will never leave my side
He will ensure
I remain in his will
Day in and day out

I can trust God when
I can't trust myself

God is good
He is our guarantee
Of life eternal
Of life abundant

Only he alone can guarantee
Not the powers of this world
Not the wealth and fame
Not the seemingly powerful
But limited strength of our adversary
The enemy of souls
The rebellion to God
The All-Sufficient One

Thank you, God, for who you are
May my soul rest in peace
Knowing you will never let me go
Your sheep know your voice
I will never be led astray
Of this, I can be confident
Not in myself but in you

God can be trusted
Yes, God can be trusted, oh my soul

Extra Poems

THE THIRTY-TWO POEMS IN this collection were written in 2019 or earlier. Thus, I want to include two extra poems here in light of the COVID-19 pandemic that ravages our world in 2020.

The first is adapted from a song lyric that I collaborated on with several brothers and sister from my church during the lockdown period we had in New Zealand. We are not songwriters; we were trying something new in response to the situation. It was a new experience for many people being restricted and "bound" at home. We want to focus on the theme of having freedom in chains and that all of us, who are in Christ, no matter our circumstances, are heading home. To our *real* eternal home, a place where our father calls.

Thank you Caleb, Christine, and Michael for inviting me to be involved in this project. I am not a musician so it was an eye-opening experience.

The second poem delivers the message that God wants to remind us at this moment in time. It is directed at both christians and non-christians. There is hope in the darkness. There is a sense of urgency, a call for all to come to know Christ.

Homebound

My heart is numb
I am feeling distant
Left behind, people pass me by

My mind is blank
I am feeling empty
All alone, in an endless moment

I am lost, there is no one around
I am captive to these heavy chains
I cannot escape this place

...

But wait, I hear
Someone whispers to me
So calm and clear, that it comforts me

The shepherd calls
He knows my name
A guiding light, in these uncertain times

...

I am called to where God is waiting
A step draws me closer to him
A vision fills my mind

Free from my chains
Free from my sins
Into his arms, I am homebound

. . .

His love is the key
Shackles fall behind me
The past is past, I am living now

His gentle embrace
Fills my heart with endless peace
I find my stride, by my father's side

. . .

I was lost, but now I am found
Renewed in him, I soar
I have found my place, my home

Free from my chains
Free from my sins
Into his arms, I am homebound

. . .

Bound for a home
On my way back to a place
Where my father calls

I am bound for a home
On my way back to a place
Where my father calls

I am bound for a home, my father's place

COVID-19

Covid-19 ruined everything
The world will no longer be the same
Whether we have lost a loved one
Or been bombarded with bad news
Or alter our behaviors

Many are gloomy
Many are frightened
Some are still in denial
Some have lost hope

The world is coming to an end
It is soon to be gathered up
As a mother gathers her chicks
As a shepherd herds the sheep

There is a chance, still
A call
A choice
Before the end comes

Like a thief
The timing is unknown
But unlike night
We are not entirely in the dark

We lit our lamps waiting, for
What was promised millenniums ago
He gives us a chance
A call
A choice

Songs List

(for A Song Poem)

1. Grace
2. Because Of Who You Are
3. I Give You My Heart
4. I Am Not Ashamed
5. To Be Like Jesus
6. Yes, Lord, Yes
7. This I Believe
8. You are
9. More
10. Greater Still
11. Worthy Of Worship
12. Praise The King
13. Forever Reign
14. Above All
15. Blessed Be Your Name
16. Jesus Messiah
17. You Are My All In All
18. Wonderful, Merciful Savior
19. No Longer Slaves
20. I Will Rise
21. Like Eagles
22. Trust In You
23. I Want To Be Just Like You

Songs List

24. Carry The Light
25. Build A Bridge Of Love
26. Freely, Freely
27. By Faith
28. For The Glory Of The Lord
29. You Are Holy
30. Awesome God
31. Draw Me Close To You
32. Lead Me To The Cross
33. In Christ Alone
34. I Will Stand
35. Solid Rock
36. Unshakeable
37. Your Love Never Fails
38. I Can Only Imagine
39. What Faith Can Do
40. In The Name Of The Lord

www.ingramcontent.com/pod-product-compliance
Lightning Source LLC
Chambersburg PA
CBHW071743040426
42446CB00012B/2462